EXPLORING THE HUMAN BODY

The Skeleton and Muscles

Carol Ballard

KIDHAVEN PRESS

An imprint of Thomson Gale, a part of The Thomson Corporation

THOMSON

GALE

Detroit • New York • San Francisco • San Diego • New Haven, Conn. • Waterville, Maine • London • Munich

THOMSON

™

GALE

Produced by Arcturus Publishing Ltd,
26/27 Bickels Yard, 151–153 Bermondsey Street, London SE1 3HA

© 2005 Arcturus Publishing

The right of Carol Ballard to be identified as the author of this work has been asserted by her in accordance with the Copyright, Designs and Patents Act 1988.

Series concept: Alex Woolf
Editor: Alex Woolf
Designer: Peta Morey
Artwork: Michael Courtney
Picture researcher: Glass Onion Pictures
Consultant: Dr Kristina Routh

Thomson and Star Logo are trademarks and Gale and KidHaven Press are registered trademarks used herein under license.

For more information, contact
KidHaven Press
27500 Drake Rd.
Farmington Hills, MI 48331-3535
Or you can visit our Internet site at http://www.gale.com

Picture Credits
Science Photo Library: 5 (Tony McConnell), 7 (Department of Clinical Radiology, Salisbury District Hospital), 9 (CNRI), 11 (Hattie Young), 13 (D. Roberts), 15 (Oscar Burriel), 17 (Zephyr), 23 (BSIP / Chassenet), 25 (Coneyl Jay), 27 (BSIP, Barrelle), 28 (Sheila Terry).
Topfoto: 18, 20, 29 (David Wimsett / UPPA).

LIBRARY OF CONGRESS CATALOGING-IN-PUBLICATION DATA

Ballard, Carol.
  The skeleton and muscles / by Carol Ballard.
    p. cm. — (Exploring the human body)
  Includes bibliographical references and index.
  ISBN 0-7377-3022-6 (hardcover : alk. paper)
    1. Musculoskeletal system—Juvenile literature. I. Title. II. Series.
  QP301.B317 2005
  611'.7—dc22

                                                    2004023217

Printed in Singapore

Contents

What Are Skeletons and Muscles?   4

Inside a Bone   6

Bone Shapes   8

Joints   10

Face and Head   12

Back   14

Chest   16

Shoulders, Arms, and Hands   18

Hips, Legs, and Feet   20

What Are Muscles?   22

Different Muscles   24

Pulling Bones   26

Taking Care of Bones and Muscles   28

Glossary   30

For Further Exploration   31

Index   32

What Are Skeletons and Muscles?

Your skeleton of bones is a framework that supports the rest of your body. It protects internal organs, allows you to move, and gives your body its shape.

There are 206 bones in your skeleton. Some of these are made up of smaller bones joined together. Each bone is exactly the right shape, size, and strength for the job it has to do. For example, your thigh bones are long and straight, giving your legs their shape. They are also very strong, to carry the weight of your body.

Your skeleton has several main parts. The bones of your head and face make up your skull. A bony column called your spine runs down the center of your back. Your chest is made from the bones of your rib cage. Your arms and hands hang from a bony crossbar called the pectoral girdle. Your legs and feet hang from a ring of bone called the pelvic girdle.

The places where two or more bones meet are called **joints**. Knees, ankles, elbows, and wrists are all

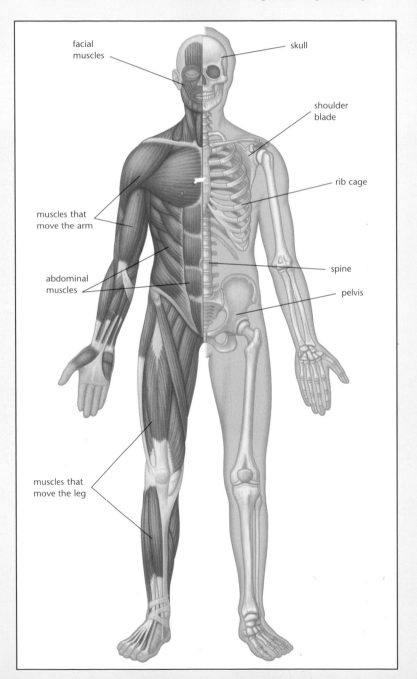

facial muscles

skull

shoulder blade

rib cage

muscles that move the arm

abdominal muscles

spine

pelvis

muscles that move the leg

joints. Tough **fibers** called **ligaments** hold the bones together at each joint. They also allow the bones to move past each other. This lets you bend and move parts of your body.

Bones cannot move by themselves. They have to be pulled into new positions by stretchy bands called muscles. Some muscles, such as those that move your thigh bones, are powerful and allow large movements. Other muscles are tiny, such as those that control the movements of your eyeballs. Besides moving your bones, muscles also help you keep your balance and stay upright.

You can see the shapes of this man's muscles under his skin.

Not all muscles are attached to bones. Some, like those around your mouth, are attached to skin. Others carry out important jobs inside your body, such as to help food pass along your **digestive system**, and to allow you to breathe. Your **heart** is the most important muscle in your body. It pumps blood around your body every minute of every day, whether you are awake or asleep.

Case notes

What would I be like without a skeleton?

Your skeleton gives your body its shape. Without it, you would just be a shapeless, jellylike blob! You would not be able to move around, as there would be no bones for the muscles to pull. You would not be able to pick anything up, kick a ball, or ride a bicycle. In fact, you wouldn't really be able to do anything at all!

Inside a Bone

We might think of bones as solid objects, but they are not as simple as that. They are made up of several different layers, complete with a blood supply and **nerves**. Their structure makes them strong and light.

Most bones have a tough outer layer that contains nerves and **blood vessels**. Inside this is a strong, hard layer made of a material called **compact bone**. Blood vessels and nerves run through holes in the compact bone to the inner layer, called **spongy bone**. Spongy bone is a mesh of bone pieces. A soft jelly called **bone marrow** fills the spaces between them. Red bone marrow, found at the ends of bones, helps produce red blood cells. Yellow bone marrow, found in the middle areas of bones, is mainly fat.

This diagram shows the layers inside a bone.

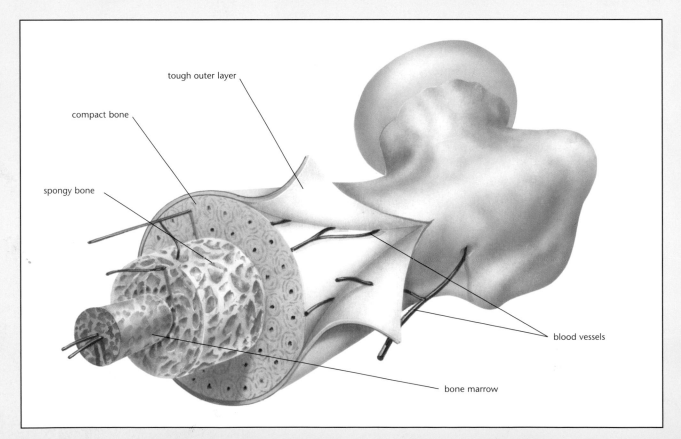

tough outer layer

compact bone

spongy bone

blood vessels

bone marrow

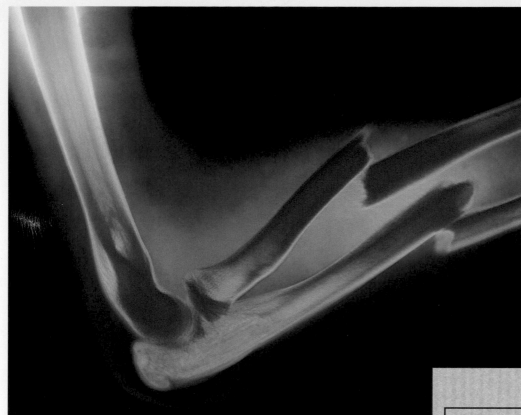

This X-ray shows broken bones in the lower arm.

Bones are living tissues, just like the rest of your body. The blood vessels running through the bones bring **oxygen** and **nutrients** for the bones to use. They also carry away waste that the bones produce. Bones need to communicate with the **brain**. The nerves in the bones carry information to the brain about bone pain or damage.

Nearly three-fourths of bone material is made up of **minerals** such as calcium, phosphorus, magnesium, and zinc. These minerals make the bone hard. In young children, the bones are slightly soft and flexible, but they become stronger and harder as more minerals are deposited. Bones keep their full strength for most of an adult's life. In older people, though, some minerals may be lost from bones, making them weaker and easier to break.

Bones act as a mineral store for the body. If your body has plenty of calcium, your bones will store any that is not needed. If there is too little calcium, your bones will release some for use by other parts of your body.

Case notes

What happens when a bone gets broken?

Just as your body is able to grow new skin to heal a cut, it can grow new bone to heal a broken bone. Doctors make sure that the broken parts of the bone are in a straight line and then wrap them in plaster to keep them from moving. Slowly, new bone forms at the broken ends and the bone joins back together. This may take a few weeks, or even months if a large bone is badly broken.

Bone Shapes

Bones come in a variety of different shapes and sizes, depending on their position in the body and the job they have to do. There are five main bone shapes:

- **Long bones** are long and nearly straight. The bones in your arms and legs are long bones. They are strong and often act as levers. These bones play an important part in moving your body.
- **Short bones** are small and roughly cube shaped. The bones in your wrists and ankles are short bones. They can slide easily past each other, making these joints flexible.
- **Flat bones** are thin, curved bones. The ribs, breastbone, shoulder blades, and some skull bones are all flat bones. Their shape makes them strong so they can provide protection for other parts of your body. For example, your skull protects your brain. Your ribs and breastbone protect your heart and **lungs**.
- **Irregular bones** come in all sorts of shapes. The bones of your face and spine are all irregular bones.

This picture shows where different types of bones are found in the human body.

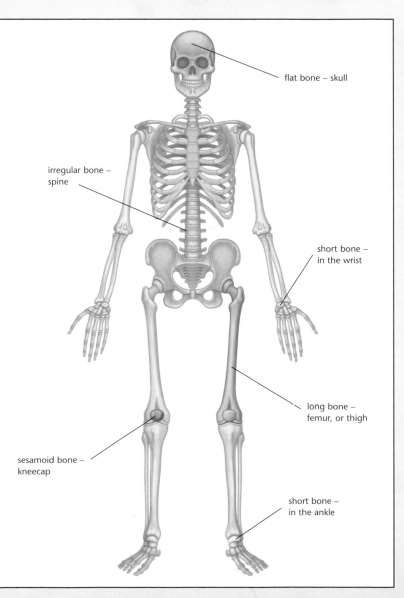

flat bone – skull

irregular bone – spine

short bone – in the wrist

long bone – femur, or thigh

sesamoid bone – kneecap

short bone – in the ankle

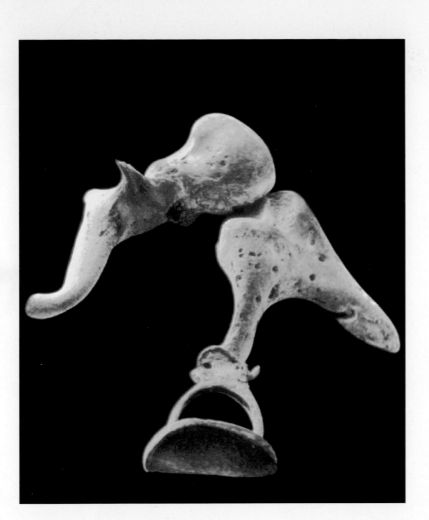

These tiny, irregular bones link together inside your ear to carry sound vibrations.

- **Sesamoid bones** get their name from being shaped like sesame seeds. They are found at joints and help make the joint work smoothly. The kneecap is a sesamoid bone.

People do not all have the same number of bones. When a baby is born, it may have 300 bones. During childhood, many bones join together, making the 206 bones of most adult skeletons. Some bones may not join completely, and so extra bones are left. These are called accessory bones and are most often found in the feet. A baby's skull bones are separate when it is born and slowly join together to form the skull. The joints between these bones are called **sutures**. Small accessory bones, known as sutural bones, may be found between these joints.

Case notes

How do bones grow?

As we grow from babies into children and teenagers, we all get bigger. This means that, along with the rest of our bodies, our bones have to grow. At each end of a bone is a special area called a growth plate. This makes new bone material on its inside edge, so the bone slowly gets larger. The growth plate stops making new bone material when you have reached your full adult size.

Joints

A joint is a place where two or more bones meet. Here, the bones can move easily past each other, allowing you to move parts of your body.

Most joints are covered by a ligament layer called a capsule. Inside this is a thin layer called a **synovial membrane**. This makes a special fluid that makes the joint slippery, so that the bones can move easily. The end of each bone is covered with a protective layer of **cartilage**, a stiff, rubbery material. The bones are held firmly in place by strong bands of ligaments. These allow the bones to move, but keep them from slipping too far apart.

Hinge joints

Elbows and knees are examples of hinge joints. They get their name because they work like a simple hinge, allowing movement in one direction only. To see how these work, hold your arm straight out in front of you with your palm turned upwards. Imagine your lower arm is a door and your upper arm is the fixed doorframe. If you keep your upper arm absolutely still, you can only move your lower arm backwards and forwards, just like a door opening and closing. You cannot bend it from side to side or around in a circle.

Each picture shows a different type of joint.

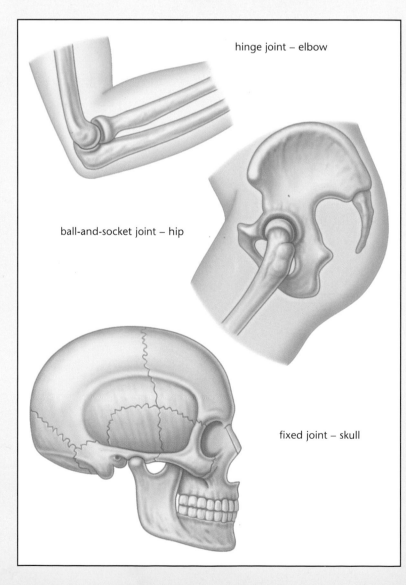

hinge joint – elbow

ball-and-socket joint – hip

fixed joint – skull

Ball-and-socket joints

Shoulders and hips are examples of ball-and-socket joints. These large, strong joints allow much more movement than hinge joints. The joints get their name from the shapes of the bones. One bone has a round, ball-shaped end. This fits snugly into the cup-shaped end of the other bone. In the hip, the ball-shaped top of the thigh bone fits into a cup in the pelvic girdle. The ball can rotate inside the cup, allowing you to move your thigh up and down, backwards and forwards, and from side to side.

A nurse winds a bandage around a sprained ankle. The injury may be painful, but it will soon heal.

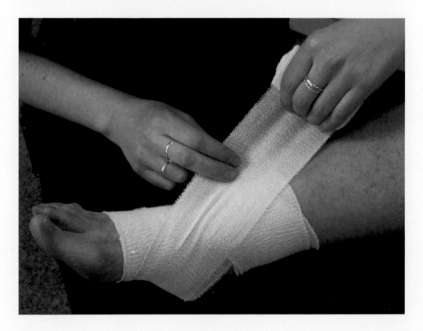

There are other types of joints, too:

- fixed joints, such as those between skull bones, which allow no movement
- saddle joints, like the joint between the thumb and wrist, which allow movement in all directions
- gliding joints, like those in the ankle, which allow bones to slide over each other
- condyloid joints, like the knuckles, which allow movement up and down as well as side to side
- pivot joints, like that at the base of the skull, which allow bones to rotate.

Case notes

What is a sprain?

A **sprain** is an injury to the ligaments of a joint that occurs when the joint is stretched or twisted too far. If a joint is sprained, it feels very sore and may be swollen. A sprained wrist is often so sore that the hand movement is limited. A sprained ankle is often too sore to stand on. Sprained joints need to be rested, and an ice pack may help to reduce swelling. Most sprains get better within a few days, although a bad sprain may take much longer.

Face and Head

There are two main parts to your skull: your cranium, which is the round part of your skull, and your face, which forms the front part of your skull. Although we usually think of the skull as being one piece of bone, it is actually made up of twenty-two bones. There are seven other bones in your head as well. There are three tiny bones inside each ear, and a bone that supports your tongue, helping you speak and swallow.

Here you can see how the bones of the skull fit together.

Cranium

Your cranium is made up of eight bones joined together like jigsaw pieces. The joints, called sutures, are held together by strong fibers. One large bone (frontal bone) forms the forehead and the tops of the eye sockets. Two large bones (parietal bones) and two smaller bones (temporal bones) form the sides of the head, and a single large bone (occipital bone) forms the back of the head. A single bone (ethmoid bone) forms the inside of the nose and other internal parts of the head. The whole structure is held together by a single bone (sphenoid bone) that stretches across the inside of the head from one side to the other.

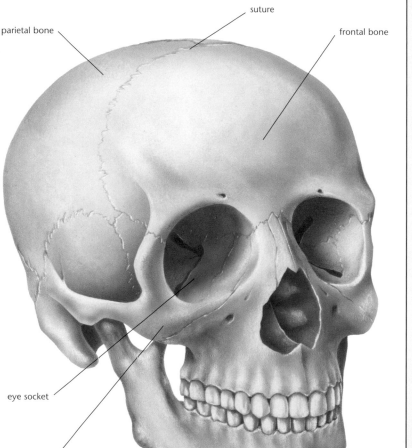

parietal bone

suture

frontal bone

eye socket

cheek bone

lower jaw

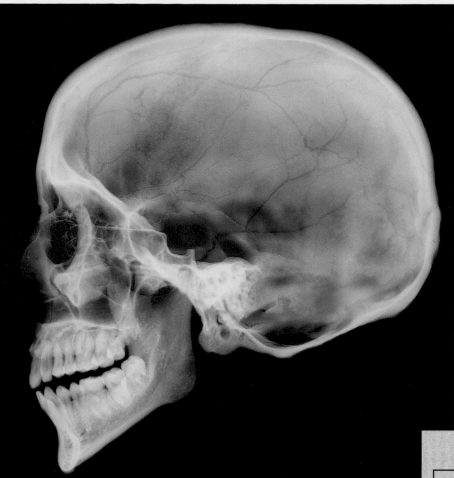

This is an X-ray of a human skull. The light areas are bone and the dark areas are spaces.

Face

Your face is made up of fourteen bones. Thirteen are joined together and cannot move. Together they form the lower part of your eye sockets, the ridge of your cheeks, and your upper jaw. The other bone is your lower jawbone (mandible), which is linked to the fixed face bones by a hinge joint at each side. This allows you to move your lower jaw up and down so that you can talk and chew. The bones of the face are not all solid. Some have hollow spaces inside them called sinuses. These are filled with air and have a thin lining that produces a fluid called mucus. Sinuses are important when you talk and sing, because they help make your voice sound louder. If you have a bad cold or an infection, the sinuses may become blocked. This is called sinusitis and it can cause a headache.

Case notes

Why isn't there a nose bone on the skull?

If you look at a picture of a human skull you will see that there is a hole where the nose should be. This is because most of the nose has no bone. Two small bones between the eyes form the bridge of the nose. The main part of the nose is stiffened with a piece of cartilage instead of bone.

Back

Your backbone, or spine, runs from the base of your skull down the center of your back, providing an upright support for the rest of your body. It is made up of a column of thirty-three separate bones stacked one on top of the other. Disks of cartilage in between the bones cushion and protect them so they can move without rubbing together. Each bone is called a vertebra. Another name for the spine is the vertebral column. The vertebrae and cartilage disks fit together and are held in place by muscles, **tendons**, and ligaments.

The vertebrae can be thought of in groups. The top seven vertebrae make up the neck and are called cervical vertebrae. Below these are the twelve thoracic vertebrae that make up the back of the chest. Then come five strong lumbar vertebrae that support the powerful back muscles. The five sacral vertebrae below these are separate in children but slowly join together to make one bone called the sacrum. Right at the bottom of the spine is the coccyx, a tiny tailbone made from the joining together of the last four vertebrae.

Your spine is not absolutely straight. It is a slightly curved "S" shape. This curve helps to keep your body weight evenly balanced. It also helps make the spine stronger. The structure of the spine makes it flexible, allowing you to bend backward and forward, up and down, from side to side, and around in a twist.

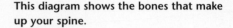
This diagram shows the bones that make up your spine.

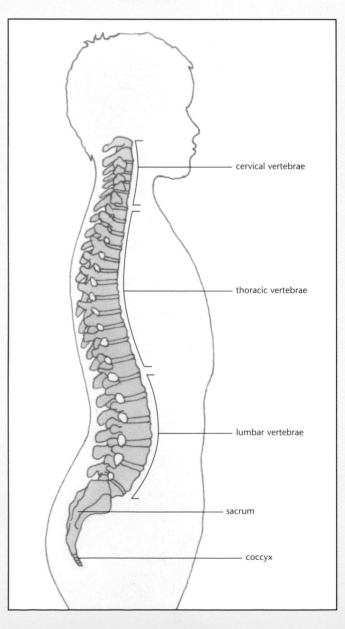

cervical vertebrae

thoracic vertebrae

lumbar vertebrae

sacrum

coccyx

The human spine is strong and flexible, allowing us to bend and stretch in different directions.

Each of the vertebrae is a slightly different shape from the ones above and below it, but they all have the same basic structure. A strong, solid piece of bone, called the body, faces the front of your body. Other pieces of bone, called processes, stick out at the back and sides. Some processes help the vertebra stay in place. Others have muscles attached. The body and processes together form a ring of bone.

As the vertebrae are stacked on top of each other, these rings are lined up, with a hollow space running right down the middle of them. This space provides a safe, strong channel for a bundle of nerves called the **spinal cord**. This runs down the central space, connecting the brain to the rest of the body. If the spinal cord is damaged, the link between the brain and other parts of the body may be broken, resulting in **paralysis**.

Case notes

What is a slipped disk?

When you stand up normally, the disks between the vertebrae are squashed. Bending awkwardly or lifting heavy objects can cause a disk to become squashed more on one side than on the other. Part of the disk may jut out from between the vertebrae and be very painful if it presses against the spinal nerves. Resting, gentle exercise, and heat treatment often help. In some cases, doctors may operate to remove the damaged disk completely.

Chest

Your chest is made up of a set of twelve pairs of ribs, together with your upper spine at the back and your collarbones and breastbone at the front. These bones are held in place by muscles and pieces of cartilage. Together, this whole structure is called your rib cage.

Your rib cage has two very important jobs to do. First, it provides a strong, bony cage to protect your heart and lungs. Secondly, it allows you to breathe in and out.

The breastbone, or sternum, is a long, flat bone that has three parts. The top part has a notch on each side for the ends of the collarbones to fit into. The top pair of ribs are also attached to this part of the sternum. Below this is a longer piece of bone, to which the rest of the ribs are attached. The small, pointed bottom piece of the sternum is made of cartilage in children, but hardens into bone in middle age.

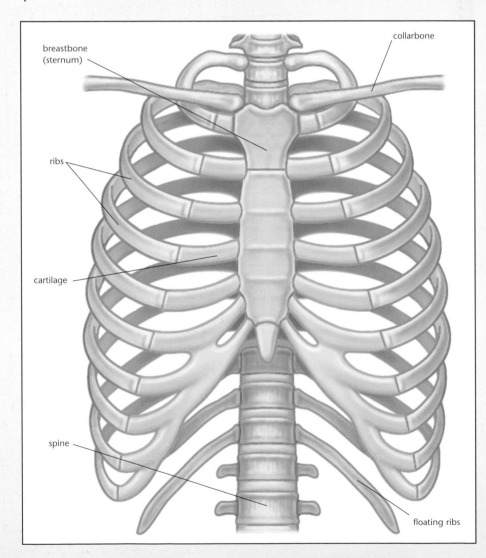

breastbone (sternum)

collarbone

ribs

cartilage

spine

floating ribs

The bones of the rib cage showing the attachments to the sternum and spine.

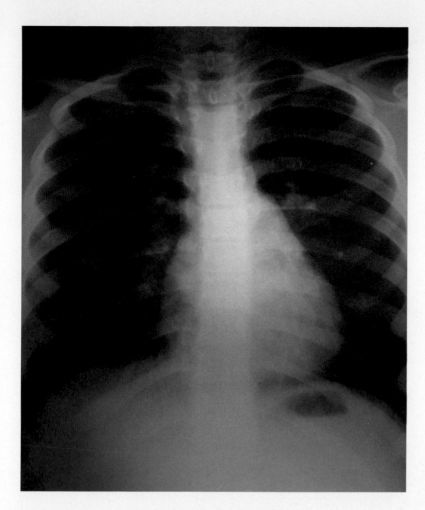

This colored X-ray shows the heart within the rib cage.

Ribs are curved, flat bones. At the back of the rib cage, each rib is attached to a vertebra. At the front, the top seven pairs of ribs are attached to the sternum by strips of cartilage. The next three pairs are linked together by a single piece of cartilage, which is in turn linked to the sternum. The bottom two pairs of ribs are not linked to the sternum at all and are called floating ribs.

Accidents such as falling heavily or a hard blow to the chest can result in broken ribs. This can be painful but is not usually dangerous. Broken ribs are often left to heal on their own. The chest may be bandaged to prevent further damage. An operation may sometimes be needed, especially if doctors think the broken ribs may damage the heart or lungs.

Case notes

How does my rib cage help me breathe?

When you breathe in, muscles attached to your ribs lift your ribs upward and outward. This makes the space inside your chest bigger so that air is sucked into your lungs. When you breathe out, the opposite happens. Muscles let your ribs move downward and inward so that waste gas is pushed out of your lungs.

Shoulders, Arms, and Hands

Your arms hang down from a horizontal bony crossbar called the pectoral girdle. This is made up of your shoulder blades (scapulae) at the back and the collarbones (clavicles) at the front. The shoulder blades are held in place by powerful muscles. Ligaments attach your collarbones to the sternum in the center of your chest and to the shoulder blades at each side.

Your shoulder joints, which link your arms to your shoulder blades, are ball-and-socket joints. These allow your arms to move freely up and down, from side to side, forward and backward, and in a full circle.

Each upper arm has a single long bone called the humerus. The rounded top ends fit into the sockets in the shoulder blades. At the lower end of each humerus is the elbow, a hinge joint that links the upper arm to the lower arm. Your elbows only allow movement in one direction.

Your lower arm has two bones, called the radius and the ulna. These can rotate around each other, allowing you to turn your hands over and back. They are connected to each other by strong fibers.

Your lower arm bones end at your wrist joints. These joints each contain eight small bones. They can slide past each other, so you can move your wrist in any direction.

Your shoulder joint allows your arm to swing freely when you throw a ball.

Each hand has an amazing nineteen bones! The flat part of your hand has five long bones, one leading from the wrist to each finger and the thumb. Each finger has three long bones, and the thumbs each have two bones. The joints between the finger bones are hinge joints, allowing you to bend your fingers up and down. The joint at the

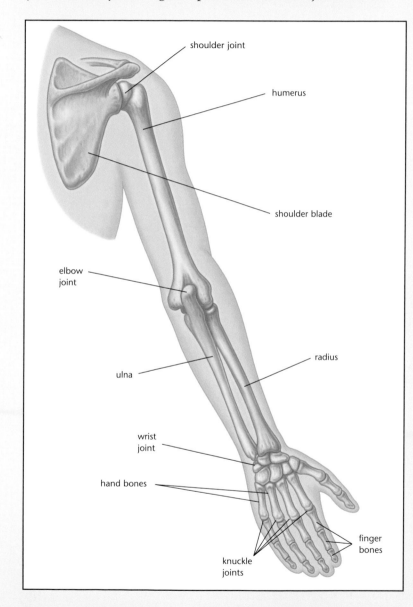

shoulder joint

humerus

shoulder blade

elbow joint

ulna

radius

wrist joint

hand bones

knuckle joints

finger bones

Here you can see how the bones are arranged in your arm and hand.

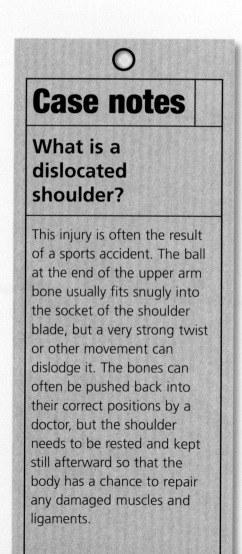

Case notes

What is a dislocated shoulder?

This injury is often the result of a sports accident. The ball at the end of the upper arm bone usually fits snugly into the socket of the shoulder blade, but a very strong twist or other movement can dislodge it. The bones can often be pushed back into their correct positions by a doctor, but the shoulder needs to be rested and kept still afterward so that the body has a chance to repair any damaged muscles and ligaments.

base of each thumb is a saddle joint, allowing you to rotate your thumb in all directions. This means you can pick things up between your finger and thumb, something that only humans and some apes can do.

Hips, Legs, and Feet

Your legs hang down from a strong, bony ring called the pelvis. This is made up of your sacrum and coccyx at the back and the hip bones at the front and sides. These bones are held in place by ligaments, and have powerful muscles attached to them.

Your hip joints, linking your legs to your pelvis, are ball-and-socket joints. They allow your legs to move freely up and down, from side to side, forward and backward, and in a full circle. Although the structure of the hip joints is similar to that of the shoulder joints, your legs cannot move quite as freely as your arms. This is because the strong ligaments that hold each hip joint together limit its movement to prevent dislocation.

Strong thigh bones carry the full weight of your body when you run.

Your thighs each have one long bone, called the femur. These are the biggest, strongest bones in your body, and support your full weight. In most adults, these bones are about one-fourth of the person's full height. The femurs are linked to your lower legs at the knee joints. These are hinge joints that only allow you to move your lower legs in an up-and-down direction. At the front of each knee joint is a small bone called the kneecap, or patella, which protects the joint.

Each lower leg has two bones, called the tibia and the fibula. Strong fibers connect these bones to each other. The tibia is much stronger than the fibula and is connected to the lower end of the thigh bone and to the ankle. The weaker fibula is linked to the top of the tibia and to the ankle.

Your lower leg bones end at your ankles. These joints

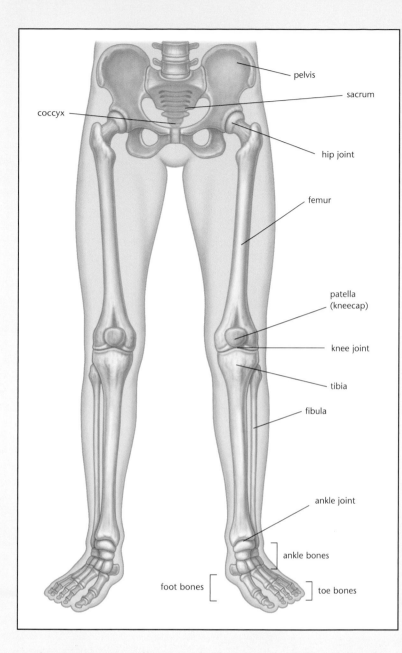

pelvis

sacrum

coccyx

hip joint

femur

patella
(kneecap)

knee joint

tibia

fibula

ankle joint

ankle bones

foot bones

toe bones

In this diagram, you can see how the bones in your legs are arranged.

each contain seven bones, which carry the full weight of your body.

The long central part of each foot has five long bones, one leading from the ankle to each toe. Each big toe has two long bones and the other toes each have three long bones. Just as in your hands, the joints between the toe bones are hinge joints, allowing you to bend your toes up and down. The toes are very important in helping you to balance. They are much shorter than your fingers, and cannot make such precise movements.

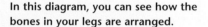

Case notes

How do doctors replace hips?

Bones can become weak and joints can become damaged and painful as people get older. If a hip joint is damaged, doctors may decide to replace it with an artificial one. The ball of the thigh bone and the socket of the hip bone are removed. A metal joint is inserted in their place. A metal shaft holds the joint into the thigh bone, and a metal or plastic cup is screwed into the hip bone. The new joint allows the person to move the hip easily again.

What Are Muscles?

Muscles that help you move your body are called **skeletal** muscles. You can control how they move—for example, you can choose how high to lift your foot, when to nod or shake your head, and which fingers to use to play a piano. Muscles that you can control are called voluntary muscles. These muscles make up more than one-third of an adult's body weight.

Skeletal muscle is made up of long, thin strands called fibers. These are bound into bundles, which are held together by an outer layer. Blood vessels run in between the bundles of fibers. These vessels bring oxygen and nutrients that the muscle needs, and carry away waste chemicals made by the muscle. Nerves are also attached to muscle fibers. These carry messages between the brain and the muscle.

Muscles are made up of bundles of fibers.

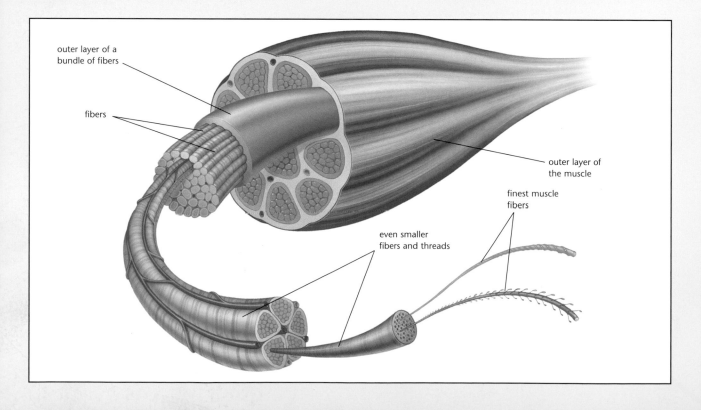

outer layer of a
bundle of fibers

fibers

outer layer of
the muscle

finest muscle
fibers

even smaller
fibers and threads

This man is flexing his biceps muscle. If you put one hand on your upper arm and make a fist with your other hand, you should feel your biceps move when you lift your fist!

To move part of your body, your brain sends a signal to a skeletal muscle telling it to **contract**. To do this, tiny threads inside the muscle fibers slide past each other, making the whole muscle shorter and fatter. To understand how this works, imagine several pencils laid end to end in a long, thin line. If you slide them along so that all the ends are together, you end up with a shorter, fatter bundle.

Most skeletal muscles are attached to bones by tendons. These are strong cords, attached at one end to the muscle and at the other end to the bone. The thickest tendon in your body is the Achilles tendon, which attaches your calf muscle to your heel bone.

There are other important types of muscles as well, which you cannot control. One is **cardiac** muscle, which your heart is made of. This is very strong muscle and operates continuously throughout your life. Smooth muscle is another type of muscle you cannot control. It forms part of the walls of your digestive organs and helps food move along your digestive system. **Artery** walls also contain smooth muscle to help control blood flow.

Case notes

What happens when I get a cramp?

Most people will have felt the sharp, stabbing pain of a **cramp** at some time. It happens when a muscle contracts tightly and does not relax. There are several different causes of cramps, including a lack of salt, too little water, and poor blood flow. Sometimes, though, cramps just seem to happen for no reason at all. Gently rubbing the muscle and slowly moving the affected part of your body can help to ease a cramp.

Different Muscles

Skeletal muscles come in a variety of shapes and sizes, depending on the job they have to do. Some are tiny and make very small, precise movements. Others are strong and powerful and are able to make large movements. Muscles can be grouped according to their shape.

Simple muscles are thin and not very strong. Bundles of muscle fibers run along the length of the muscle. A muscle like this moves the hyoid bone in your throat when you talk and swallow. Some muscles in your abdomen are also like this.

Some muscles are fat in the middle, with a strong tendon at each end to attach the muscle to neighboring bones. Again, bundles of muscle fibers run along the length of the muscle. The biceps muscle in your upper arm is like this. It contracts to lift your lower arm.

Some muscles have shorter bundles of fibers that fan out from a central tendon. These muscles can be very strong. The bundles of fibers can be arranged in a straight line or a triangular shape, or spread out into a fan shape. Straight muscles allow you to move fingers and toes. The muscles around your shoulder

Muscles come in a range of sizes and shapes.

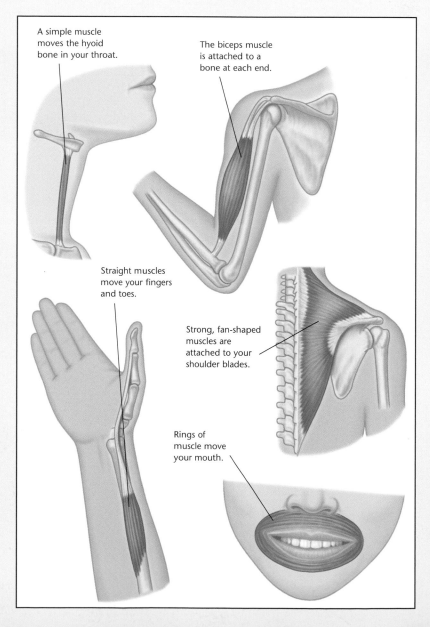

A simple muscle moves the hyoid bone in your throat.

The biceps muscle is attached to a bone at each end.

Straight muscles move your fingers and toes.

Strong, fan-shaped muscles are attached to your shoulder blades.

Rings of muscle move your mouth.

Muscles in your face allow you to smile or frown.

blades are powerful, fan-shaped muscles. Across your chest, strong triangular muscles are attached to your collarbones, breastbone, ribs, and upper arm bone.

Skeletal muscles are not only attached to bone. Your face has more than thirty muscles. Some are attached to skin as well as bone. They contract to allow you to frown, smile, and make all sorts of expressions.

In some parts of your body, muscles are arranged in rings. These control the size of openings. Rings of muscle control your lips and the **iris** of your eye. They also control openings from your **bladder** and digestive system that you use when you get rid of body waste.

Case notes

Why are some people paralyzed?

When you want to move, signals travel along nerves from your brain to your muscles. These signals make the muscles contract and move your body. If there is a problem with the nerves, the signals cannot reach the muscles. So the muscles do not contract and the body does not move. This is called paralysis and a person suffering from it is said to be paralyzed. Paralysis is often the result of an accident in which the spinal cord is damaged.

Pulling Bones

Bones are moved by muscles. When you decide to move a bone, one or more muscles attached to it contract (get shorter). This pulls the bone into a new position. Muscles can only pull bones. They cannot push them. To move a bone back again, it has to be pulled by another muscle. For this reason, muscles work in pairs, with each muscle in the pair having an opposite effect to the other.

You can see how a pair of muscles works if you think about raising and lowering your lower arm. To raise your lower arm, your biceps muscle at the front of your upper arm contracts, pulling the bone upward. This stretches the triceps muscle at the back of your upper arm. To lower your arm again, the triceps muscle contracts, pulling the bone downward. This stretches the biceps muscle.

Other pairs of muscles all over your body work like this, with one muscle contracting to move a bone one way, and another contracting to move it back again. For example, to bend a finger, a muscle in the palm of your hand contracts and pulls the finger bones inward. To straighten the finger, a muscle on the back of your hand contracts and pulls the bones outward.

Here you can see how paired muscles work in opposite ways to raise and lower your lower arm.

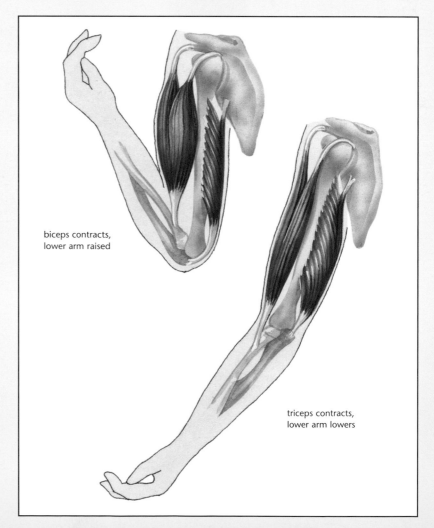

biceps contracts, lower arm raised

triceps contracts, lower arm lowers

This toddler is learning to coordinate muscle movements in order to walk.

Many of our movements are more complicated than this and involve more pairs of muscles moving several bones in more than one direction. Even a simple step forward is made up of a complex sequence of muscle movements. Many muscles pull on bones in your back and legs, helping you to keep your balance and stay upright.

To be able to make precisely the movement you want takes practice. Your brain has to send signals to coordinate all the muscles to move in the right order and at the right time.

Case notes

Fast or slow?

Your skeletal muscles contain two different types of fibers: white fibers and red fibers. These do different things. White fibers do not have a good blood supply. They use up their supply of energy very quickly and waste products build up. They soon become tired. White fibers can contract very quickly for short periods, so they are important for short, fast activities such as sprinting. Red fibers have a good blood supply that brings energy and oxygen and carries away waste products. They do not become tired quickly. Red fibers contract more slowly but can keep going for a longer time, so they are important for activities that last longer, such as cross-country and marathon running.

Taking Care of Bones and Muscles

Your bones and muscles are very important, so it makes sense to take good care of them. There are some simple things that you can do to make sure your bones and muscles are strong and safe.

Your body uses the food you eat for raw material to build bones and muscles. A balanced diet, containing fresh fruits and vegetables and protein foods such as meat, fish, eggs, and nuts, will provide all the building blocks your body needs. Starchy foods, such as wholegrain bread, pasta, and rice provide energy for muscles to use. You lose water when you sweat, so it is important to drink plenty, especially in hot weather and when you exercise.

A balanced diet helps to build strong bones and muscles.

Exercise helps muscles and bones become stronger, so the more you exercise, the fitter and healthier your body will be. It is a good idea to exercise every day. Swimming, dancing, cycling, and team games are all good exercise for your muscles and bones.

Some sports involve risks. It makes sense to reduce these risks as much as you can. One way to do this is to wear the correct protective clothing for your sport. Horseback riders wear helmets and often body protectors too. Skateboarders often wear protective pads on their elbows and knees. Cyclists should always wear a protective helmet when riding their bikes.

Your everyday lifestyle can affect your bones and muscles. Sitting up straight is much better for the muscles

Wearing the right protective gear for sports can help prevent injuries.

and bones of your back than slouching lazily on a sofa. Carrying a backpack in the middle of your back instead of over one shoulder spreads the weight evenly over both shoulders, rather than having it on just one side. Bending at the knees to lift a heavy weight puts less strain on your back than just bending from the waist.

○

Case notes

Why do I need to warm up before I exercise?

Warming up prepares your bones and muscles for exercise. The fluid inside your joints is gel-like when it is cold. It becomes runnier when it is warmer. You are less likely to damage a warm joint than a cold one, so gentle stretching and flexing of muscles before exercise help to avoid injury. A few gentle stretches after your workout is a good idea too, to help you avoid feeling stiff and achy later.

Glossary

artery	A large blood vessel that carries blood from the heart.
bladder	The sac that stores urine.
blood vessels	Tubes that carry blood through the body.
bone marrow	A jellylike substance inside bones.
brain	The organ that controls every part of the body.
cardiac	Having to do with the heart.
cartilage	A rubbery material that protects bones.
compact bone	The hard layer of a bone.
contract	Get shorter.
cramp	An unwanted muscle contraction.
digestive system	The organs that break down and absorb food.
fibers	Thin strands.
heart	The organ that pumps blood around the body.
iris	The colored part of the eye.
joints	The places where two or more bones meet.
ligaments	Strong bands that hold joints together.
lungs	Organs used in breathing.
minerals	Chemicals needed in tiny amounts to maintain health.
nerves	Parts of the body that carry signals to and from the brain.
nutrients	The parts of food that our bodies can use.
oxygen	A gas that is needed by every part of the body.

paralysis	A loss of the ability to move.
skeletal	Having to do with the skeleton.
spinal cord	The bundle of nerves inside the spinal column.
spongy bone	The inside layer of a bone.
sprain	An injury to a joint's ligaments.
sutures	Joints between two skull bones.
synovial membrane	The layer that produces a slippery fluid at a joint.
tendons	Strong cords that attach muscles to bones.

For Further Exploration

Books

DK Guide to the Human Body
(Dorling Kindersley, 2004)

Look at Your Body: Muscles by Steve Parker
(Franklin Watts, 1997)

My Healthy Body: Muscles by Jen Green
(Franklin Watts, 2003)

My Healthy Body: Skeleton by Jen Green
(Franklin Watts, 2003)

The Oxford Children's A to Z of the Human Body by Bridget and Neil Ardley (Oxford University Press, 2003)

Under the Microscope: Muscles
by Clive Gregory (Franklin Watts, 2001)

Under the Microscope: Skeleton by J. Johnson
(Franklin Watts, 2001)

Usborne Internet-Linked Complete Book of the Human Body by Anna Claybourne
(Usborne Publishing, 2003)

Web Sites

Human Anatomy Online
www.innerbody.com
Click on "Enter Here," then click on the skeleton picture.

Skeletal System
http://yucky.kids.discovery.com/noflash/body/pg000124.html

The Big Story on Bones
http://kidshealth.org/kid/body/bones_nosw.html

Index

Page numbers in **bold** refer to illustrations.

ankle 4, 8, **8**, 11, **11**, 20, 21, **21**
arm bones 4, 7, 8, 10, 18, 19, **19**, 20, 24, **24**, 25

babies 9, **27**
balance 5, 14, 21
biceps **23**, 24, **24**, 26, **26**
blood vessels 6, **6**, 7, 30
bone
    accessory 9
    broken 7, **7**, 17
    compact 6, **6**, 30
    flat 8, **8**, 17
    irregular 8, **8**
    long 8, **8**
    sesamoid 8, 9
    short 8, **8**
    spongy, 6, **6**, 30
bone marrow 6, **6**, 30
brain 7, 8, 15, 22, 23, 25, 27, 30
breastbone. *See* sternum
breathing 5, 16, 17

cartilage 10, 13, 14, 16, 17, 30
chest 4, 14, 16–17, 25
coccyx 14, **14**, 20, **21**
collarbone 16, 18, 25
cramp 23, 30
cranium 12

diet 28, **28**
digestive system 5, 23, 25, 30
dislocated shoulder 19

ear bones **9**, 12
elbow 4, 10, **10**, 18, **19**
ethmoid bone 12
exercise 28–29

eye socket 12, **12**

face 4, 8, 12, 13, 25, **25**
facial muscles **4**
feet 4, 9, 21, **21**, 22
femur 20, **21**
fibula 20, **21**

hands 4, 11, 18, 19, **19**
heart 5, 8, 16, 17, 23, 30
hip joint **10**, 11, 20, 21, **21**
hip replacements 21
humerus 18, **19**
hyoid bone 24, **24**

joints 4–5, 8, 9, 10–11, 18, 19, 20, 21, 29, 30
    ball-and-socket 10, 11, 18, 20
    fixed **10**, 11
    hinge 10, **10**, 13, 18, 19, 20, 21
    saddle 11, 19

kneecap **8**, 9, 20, **21**
knee joint 4, 10, 20, **21**

legs 4, 8, 20
ligaments 5, 10, 11, 14, 18, 19, 20, 30
lower jaw bone **12**, 13
lungs 8, 16, 17, 30

minerals 7, 30
mouth 5, **24**
movement 4, 8, 11, 25, 26, 27
muscle **4**, 5, **5**, 14, 15, 16, 17, 18, 19, 20, 22–29
    cardiac 23, 30
    skeletal 22, 23, 27
    smooth 23
    types 24–25, **24**
    voluntary 22
muscle fiber 22, **22**, 23, 24, 27

nerves 6, 7, 15, 22, 25, 30

occipital bone 12

paralysis 15, 25
parietal bone 12, **12**
pectoral girdle 4, 18
pelvic girdle 4, 11
pelvis 4, **4**, 20, **21**
protective clothing 28–29, **29**

radius 18, **19**
rib cage 4, **4**, 16, **16**, 17, **17**
ribs 8, 16, **16**, 17, **17**, 25

sacrum 14, **14**, 20, **21**
shoulder blade 4, 18, 19, **19**, 24–25, **24**
shoulder joint 11, 18, 20
sinuses 13
skeleton 4, **4**, 5
skull 4, **4**, 8, **8**, 9, **10**, 11, 12–13, **12**, **13**, 14
slipped disk 15
sphenoid bone 12
spinal cord 15, 25, 30
spine 4, **4**, 8, **8**, 14–15, 16, **16**
sprains 11, **11**, 30
sternum 8, 16, **16**, 17, 18, 25
sutures 9, 12, **12**, 30
synovial membrane 10, 30

temporal bone 12
tendons 14, 23, 24, 30
thigh bone 4, 5, 11, 20, 21, **21**
tibia 20, **21**
triceps 26, **26**

ulna 18, **19**

vertebrae 14, **14**, 15, 17

wrist 4, 8, **8**, 11, 18, **19**